This Recipe Journal Belongs To:

Table of Contents

RECIPE   **PAGE**

RECIPE **PAGE**

RECIPE	PAGE

RECIPE **PAGE**

RECIPE NAME:

Keto ☐ Low Carb ☐ Paleo ☐ Vegetarian ☐ Vegan ☐ Dairy Free ☐ Gluten Free ☐

QTY	INGREDIENTS	RECIPE DIRECTIONS

NOTES & RECIPE REVIEW

Serves	
Prep Time	
Cook Time	
Tools	
Temp	

Total	Carbs	Fat	Protein	Cals

Recipe

RECIPE NAME:

Keto ☐ Low Carb ☐ Paleo ☐ Vegetarian ☐ Vegan ☐ Dairy Free ☐ Gluten Free ☐

QTY	INGREDIENTS	RECIPE DIRECTIONS

NOTES & RECIPE REVIEW

Serves	
Prep Time	
Cook Time	
Tools	
Temp	

Total	Carbs	Fat	Protein	Cals

Recipe

RECIPE NAME:

Keto	Low Carb	Paleo	Vegetarian	Vegan	Dairy Free	Gluten Free
☐	☐	☐	☐	☐	☐	☐

QTY	INGREDIENTS	RECIPE DIRECTIONS

NOTES & RECIPE REVIEW

Serves	
Prep Time	
Cook Time	
Tools	
Temp	

Total	Carbs	Fat	Protein	Cals

Recipe

4

RECIPE NAME:

Keto | Low Carb | Paleo | Vegetarian | Vegan | Dairy Free | Gluten Free
☐ | ☐ | ☐ | ☐ | ☐ | ☐ | ☐

QTY	INGREDIENTS	RECIPE DIRECTIONS

NOTES & RECIPE REVIEW

Serves	
Prep Time	
Cook Time	
Tools	
Temp	

Total	Carbs	Fat	Protein	Cals

Recipe

5

RECIPE NAME:

Keto ☐ Low Carb ☐ Paleo ☐ Vegetarian ☐ Vegan ☐ Dairy Free ☐ Gluten Free ☐

QTY	INGREDIENTS	RECIPE DIRECTIONS

NOTES & RECIPE REVIEW

Serves	
Prep Time	
Cook Time	
Tools	
Temp	

Total	Carbs	Fat	Protein	Cals

Recipe

RECIPE NAME:

Keto ☐ Low Carb ☐ Paleo ☐ Vegetarian ☐ Vegan ☐ Dairy Free ☐ Gluten Free ☐

QTY	INGREDIENTS	RECIPE DIRECTIONS

NOTES & RECIPE REVIEW

Serves	
Prep Time	
Cook Time	
Tools	
Temp	

Total	Carbs	Fat	Protein	Cals

Recipe

RECIPE NAME:
_____

- ☐ Keto
- ☐ Low Carb
- ☐ Paleo
- ☐ Vegetarian
- ☐ Vegan
- ☐ Dairy Free
- ☐ Gluten Free

QTY	INGREDIENTS

RECIPE DIRECTIONS

NOTES & RECIPE REVIEW

Serves	
Prep Time	
Cook Time	
Tools	
Temp	

Total	Carbs	Fat	Protein	Cals

RECIPE NAME:

Keto ☐   Low Carb ☐   Paleo ☐   Vegetarian ☐   Vegan ☐   Dairy Free ☐   Gluten Free ☐

QTY	INGREDIENTS

RECIPE DIRECTIONS

NOTES & RECIPE REVIEW

Serves	
Prep Time	
Cook Time	
Tools	
Temp	

Total	Carbs	Fat	Protein	Cals

Recipe

RECIPE NAME:

Keto ☐   Low Carb ☐   Paleo ☐   Vegetarian ☐   Vegan ☐   Dairy Free ☐   Gluten Free ☐

QTY	INGREDIENTS	RECIPE DIRECTIONS

NOTES & RECIPE REVIEW

Serves	
Prep Time	
Cook Time	
Tools	
Temp	

Total	Carbs	Fat	Protein	Cals

Recipe

10

RECIPE NAME:

Keto ☐ Low Carb ☐ Paleo ☐ Vegetarian ☐ Vegan ☐ Dairy Free ☐ Gluten Free ☐

QTY	INGREDIENTS

RECIPE DIRECTIONS

NOTES & RECIPE REVIEW

Serves	
Prep Time	
Cook Time	
Tools	
Temp	

Total	Carbs	Fat	Protein	Cals

Recipe

RECIPE NAME:

Keto ☐ Low Carb ☐ Paleo ☐ Vegetarian ☐ Vegan ☐ Dairy Free ☐ Gluten Free ☐

QTY	INGREDIENTS	RECIPE DIRECTIONS

NOTES & RECIPE REVIEW

Serves	
Prep Time	
Cook Time	
Tools	
Temp	

Total	Carbs	Fat	Protein	Cals

Recipe

RECIPE NAME:

Keto ☐　Low Carb ☐　Paleo ☐　Vegetarian ☐　Vegan ☐　Dairy Free ☐　Gluten Free ☐

QTY	INGREDIENTS

RECIPE DIRECTIONS

NOTES & RECIPE REVIEW

Serves	
Prep Time	
Cook Time	
Tools	
Temp	

Total	Carbs	Fat	Protein	Cals

RECIPE NAME:

	Keto	Low Carb	Paleo	Vegetarian	Vegan	Dairy Free	Gluten Free
	☐	☐	☐	☐	☐	☐	☐

QTY	INGREDIENTS	RECIPE DIRECTIONS

NOTES & RECIPE REVIEW

Serves	
Prep Time	
Cook Time	
Tools	
Temp	

Total	Carbs	Fat	Protein	Cals

Recipe

14

RECIPE NAME:

| Keto | Low Carb | Paleo | Vegetarian | Vegan | Dairy Free | Gluten Free |
| ☐ | ☐ | ☐ | ☐ | ☐ | ☐ | ☐ |

QTY	INGREDIENTS	RECIPE DIRECTIONS

NOTES & RECIPE REVIEW

Serves	
Prep Time	
Cook Time	
Tools	
Temp	

Total	Carbs	Fat	Protein	Cals

Recipe

RECIPE NAME:

Keto ☐ Low Carb ☐ Paleo ☐ Vegetarian ☐ Vegan ☐ Dairy Free ☐ Gluten Free ☐

QTY	INGREDIENTS

RECIPE DIRECTIONS

NOTES & RECIPE REVIEW

Serves	
Prep Time	
Cook Time	
Tools	
Temp	

Total	Carbs	Fat	Protein	Cals

Recipe

RECIPE NAME:

Keto ☐ Low Carb ☐ Paleo ☐ Vegetarian ☐ Vegan ☐ Dairy Free ☐ Gluten Free ☐

QTY	INGREDIENTS	RECIPE DIRECTIONS

NOTES & RECIPE REVIEW

- Serves
- Prep Time
- Cook Time
- Tools
- Temp

Total	Carbs	Fat	Protein	Cals

Recipe

RECIPE NAME:

Keto ☐   Low Carb ☐   Paleo ☐   Vegetarian ☐   Vegan ☐   Dairy Free ☐   Gluten Free ☐

QTY	INGREDIENTS	RECIPE DIRECTIONS

NOTES & RECIPE REVIEW

Serves	
Prep Time	
Cook Time	
Tools	
Temp	

Total	Carbs	Fat	Protein	Cals

RECIPE NAME:

	Keto	Low Carb	Paleo	Vegetarian	Vegan	Dairy Free	Gluten Free
	☐	☐	☐	☐	☐	☐	☐

QTY	INGREDIENTS	RECIPE DIRECTIONS

NOTES & RECIPE REVIEW

Serves	
Prep Time	
Cook Time	
Tools	
Temp	

Total	Carbs	Fat	Protein	Cals

Recipe

RECIPE NAME:

Keto ☐ Low Carb ☐ Paleo ☐ Vegetarian ☐ Vegan ☐ Dairy Free ☐ Gluten Free ☐

QTY	INGREDIENTS

RECIPE DIRECTIONS

NOTES & RECIPE REVIEW

- Serves
- Prep Time
- Cook Time
- Tools
- Temp

Total	Carbs	Fat	Protein	Cals

Recipe 20

RECIPE NAME:

Keto ☐ Low Carb ☐ Paleo ☐ Vegetarian ☐ Vegan ☐ Dairy Free ☐ Gluten Free ☐

QTY	INGREDIENTS	RECIPE DIRECTIONS

NOTES & RECIPE REVIEW

Serves	
Prep Time	
Cook Time	
Tools	
Temp	

Total	Carbs	Fat	Protein	Cals

RECIPE NAME:

Keto ☐ Low Carb ☐ Paleo ☐ Vegetarian ☐ Vegan ☐ Dairy Free ☐ Gluten Free ☐

QTY	INGREDIENTS	RECIPE DIRECTIONS

NOTES & RECIPE REVIEW

Serves	
Prep Time	
Cook Time	
Tools	
Temp	

Total	Carbs	Fat	Protein	Cals

Recipe

RECIPE NAME:

Keto ☐ Low Carb ☐ Paleo ☐ Vegetarian ☐ Vegan ☐ Dairy Free ☐ Gluten Free ☐

QTY	INGREDIENTS	RECIPE DIRECTIONS

NOTES & RECIPE REVIEW

Serves:
Prep Time:
Cook Time:
Tools:
Temp:

Total	Carbs	Fat	Protein	Cals

RECIPE NAME:

| Keto | Low Carb | Paleo | Vegetarian | Vegan | Dairy Free | Gluten Free |
| ☐ | ☐ | ☐ | ☐ | ☐ | ☐ | ☐ |

QTY	INGREDIENTS	RECIPE DIRECTIONS

NOTES & RECIPE REVIEW

Serves	
Prep Time	
Cook Time	
Tools	
Temp	

Total	Carbs	Fat	Protein	Cals

Recipe

24

RECIPE NAME:

Keto ☐   Low Carb ☐   Paleo ☐   Vegetarian ☐   Vegan ☐   Dairy Free ☐   Gluten Free ☐

QTY	INGREDIENTS	RECIPE DIRECTIONS	

NOTES & RECIPE REVIEW

Serves	
Prep Time	
Cook Time	
Tools	
Temp	

Total	Carbs	Fat	Protein	Cals

25

RECIPE NAME:

Keto ☐ Low Carb ☐ Paleo ☐ Vegetarian ☐ Vegan ☐ Dairy Free ☐ Gluten Free ☐

QTY	INGREDIENTS	RECIPE DIRECTIONS

NOTES & RECIPE REVIEW

Serves	
Prep Time	
Cook Time	
Tools	
Temp	

Total	Carbs	Fat	Protein	Cals

Recipe

RECIPE NAME:

Keto ☐ Low Carb ☐ Paleo ☐ Vegetarian ☐ Vegan ☐ Dairy Free ☐ Gluten Free ☐

QTY	INGREDIENTS	RECIPE DIRECTIONS

NOTES & RECIPE REVIEW

Serves	
Prep Time	
Cook Time	
Tools	
Temp	

Total	Carbs	Fat	Protein	Cals

Recipe

RECIPE NAME:

- ☐ Keto
- ☐ Low Carb
- ☐ Paleo
- ☐ Vegetarian
- ☐ Vegan
- ☐ Dairy Free
- ☐ Gluten Free

QTY	INGREDIENTS

RECIPE DIRECTIONS

NOTES & RECIPE REVIEW

Serves	
Prep Time	
Cook Time	
Tools	
Temp	

Total	Carbs	Fat	Protein	Cals

Recipe

RECIPE NAME:

Keto ☐ Low Carb ☐ Paleo ☐ Vegetarian ☐ Vegan ☐ Dairy Free ☐ Gluten Free ☐

QTY	INGREDIENTS	RECIPE DIRECTIONS

NOTES & RECIPE REVIEW

Serves	
Prep Time	
Cook Time	
Tools	
Temp	

Total	Carbs	Fat	Protein	Cals

RECIPE NAME:

Keto · Low Carb · Paleo · Vegetarian · Vegan · Dairy Free · Gluten Free

QTY	INGREDIENTS	RECIPE DIRECTIONS

NOTES & RECIPE REVIEW

Serves
Prep Time
Cook Time
Tools
Temp

Total	Carbs	Fat	Protein	Cals

Recipe

RECIPE NAME:

Keto ☐　Low Carb ☐　Paleo ☐　Vegetarian ☐　Vegan ☐　Dairy Free ☐　Gluten Free ☐

QTY	INGREDIENTS	RECIPE DIRECTIONS

NOTES & RECIPE REVIEW

Serves	
Prep Time	
Cook Time	
Tools	
Temp	

Total	Carbs	Fat	Protein	Cals

Recipe

31

RECIPE NAME:

| Keto | Low Carb | Paleo | Vegetarian | Vegan | Dairy Free | Gluten Free |
| ☐ | ☐ | ☐ | ☐ | ☐ | ☐ | ☐ |

QTY	INGREDIENTS	RECIPE DIRECTIONS

NOTES & RECIPE REVIEW

Serves	
Prep Time	
Cook Time	
Tools	
Temp	

Total	Carbs	Fat	Protein	Cals

Recipe

32

RECIPE NAME:

Keto ☐ Low Carb ☐ Paleo ☐ Vegetarian ☐ Vegan ☐ Dairy Free ☐ Gluten Free ☐

QTY	INGREDIENTS	RECIPE DIRECTIONS

NOTES & RECIPE REVIEW

Serves	
Prep Time	
Cook Time	
Tools	
Temp	

Total	Carbs	Fat	Protein	Cals

RECIPE NAME:

Keto ☐ Low Carb ☐ Paleo ☐ Vegetarian ☐ Vegan ☐ Dairy Free ☐ Gluten Free ☐

QTY	INGREDIENTS	RECIPE DIRECTIONS

NOTES & RECIPE REVIEW

Serves	
Prep Time	
Cook Time	
Tools	
Temp	

Total	Carbs	Fat	Protein	Cals

Recipe

RECIPE NAME:

Keto ☐ Low Carb ☐ Paleo ☐ Vegetarian ☐ Vegan ☐ Dairy Free ☐ Gluten Free ☐

QTY	INGREDIENTS	RECIPE DIRECTIONS

NOTES & RECIPE REVIEW

Serves	
Prep Time	
Cook Time	
Tools	
Temp	

Total	Carbs	Fat	Protein	Cals

RECIPE NAME:

Keto ☐   Low Carb ☐   Paleo ☐   Vegetarian ☐   Vegan ☐   Dairy Free ☐   Gluten Free ☐

QTY	INGREDIENTS	RECIPE DIRECTIONS

NOTES & RECIPE REVIEW

Serves	
Prep Time	
Cook Time	
Tools	
Temp	

Total	Carbs	Fat	Protein	Cals

Recipe

RECIPE NAME:

Keto ☐ Low Carb ☐ Paleo ☐ Vegetarian ☐ Vegan ☐ Dairy Free ☐ Gluten Free ☐

QTY	INGREDIENTS	RECIPE DIRECTIONS

NOTES & RECIPE REVIEW

Serves	
Prep Time	
Cook Time	
Tools	
Temp	

Total	Carbs	Fat	Protein	Cals

RECIPE NAME:

Keto ☐　Low Carb ☐　Paleo ☐　Vegetarian ☐　Vegan ☐　Dairy Free ☐　Gluten Free ☐

QTY	INGREDIENTS	RECIPE DIRECTIONS

NOTES & RECIPE REVIEW

Serves	
Prep Time	
Cook Time	
Tools	
Temp	

Total	Carbs	Fat	Protein	Cals

Recipe

RECIPE NAME:

Keto ☐ Low Carb ☐ Paleo ☐ Vegetarian ☐ Vegan ☐ Dairy Free ☐ Gluten Free ☐

QTY	INGREDIENTS

RECIPE DIRECTIONS

NOTES & RECIPE REVIEW

Serves	
Prep Time	
Cook Time	
Tools	
Temp	

Total	Carbs	Fat	Protein	Cals

Recipe

RECIPE NAME:

Keto ☐ Low Carb ☐ Paleo ☐ Vegetarian ☐ Vegan ☐ Dairy Free ☐ Gluten Free ☐

QTY	INGREDIENTS	RECIPE DIRECTIONS

NOTES & RECIPE REVIEW

Serves	
Prep Time	
Cook Time	
Tools	
Temp	

Total	Carbs	Fat	Protein	Cals

RECIPE NAME:

	Keto	Low Carb	Paleo	Vegetarian	Vegan	Dairy Free	Gluten Free
	☐	☐	☐	☐	☐	☐	☐

QTY	INGREDIENTS	RECIPE DIRECTIONS

NOTES & RECIPE REVIEW

Serves	
Prep Time	
Cook Time	
Tools	
Temp	

Total	Carbs	Fat	Protein	Cals

Recipe

41

RECIPE NAME:

Keto ☐ Low Carb ☐ Paleo ☐ Vegetarian ☐ Vegan ☐ Dairy Free ☐ Gluten Free ☐

QTY	INGREDIENTS	RECIPE DIRECTIONS

NOTES & RECIPE REVIEW

Serves	
Prep Time	
Cook Time	
Tools	
Temp	

Total	Carbs	Fat	Protein	Cals

Recipe

RECIPE NAME:

Keto ☐ Low Carb ☐ Paleo ☐ Vegetarian ☐ Vegan ☐ Dairy Free ☐ Gluten Free ☐

QTY	INGREDIENTS	RECIPE DIRECTIONS

NOTES & RECIPE REVIEW

Serves:
Prep Time:
Cook Time:
Tools:
Temp:

Total	Carbs	Fat	Protein	Cals

RECIPE NAME:

Keto	Low Carb	Paleo	Vegetarian	Vegan	Dairy Free	Gluten Free
☐	☐	☐	☐	☐	☐	☐

QTY	INGREDIENTS	RECIPE DIRECTIONS

NOTES & RECIPE REVIEW

Serves	
Prep Time	
Cook Time	
Tools	
Temp	

Total	Carbs	Fat	Protein	Cals

Recipe

RECIPE NAME:

Keto ☐   Low Carb ☐   Paleo ☐   Vegetarian ☐   Vegan ☐   Dairy Free ☐   Gluten Free ☐

QTY	INGREDIENTS

RECIPE DIRECTIONS

NOTES & RECIPE REVIEW

Serves	
Prep Time	
Cook Time	
Tools	
Temp	

Total	Carbs	Fat	Protein	Cals

45

RECIPE NAME:

| Keto | Low Carb | Paleo | Vegetarian | Vegan | Dairy Free | Gluten Free |
| ☐ | ☐ | ☐ | ☐ | ☐ | ☐ | ☐ |

QTY	INGREDIENTS	RECIPE DIRECTIONS

NOTES & RECIPE REVIEW

Serves	
Prep Time	
Cook Time	
Tools	
Temp	

Total	Carbs	Fat	Protein	Cals

RECIPE NAME:

Keto ☐ Low Carb ☐ Paleo ☐ Vegetarian ☐ Vegan ☐ Dairy Free ☐ Gluten Free ☐

QTY	INGREDIENTS	RECIPE DIRECTIONS

NOTES & RECIPE REVIEW

Serves	
Prep Time	
Cook Time	
Tools	
Temp	

Total	Carbs	Fat	Protein	Cals

RECIPE NAME:

Keto ☐　Low Carb ☐　Paleo ☐　Vegetarian ☐　Vegan ☐　Dairy Free ☐　Gluten Free ☐

QTY	INGREDIENTS

RECIPE DIRECTIONS

NOTES & RECIPE REVIEW

Serves	
Prep Time	
Cook Time	
Tools	
Temp	

Total	Carbs	Fat	Protein	Cals

RECIPE NAME:

Keto · Low Carb · Paleo · Vegetarian · Vegan · Dairy Free · Gluten Free

QTY	INGREDIENTS

RECIPE DIRECTIONS

NOTES & RECIPE REVIEW

Serves	
Prep Time	
Cook Time	
Tools	
Temp	

Total	Carbs	Fat	Protein	Cals

48

49

RECIPE NAME:

Keto ☐   Low Carb ☐   Paleo ☐   Vegetarian ☐   Vegan ☐   Dairy Free ☐   Gluten Free ☐

QTY	INGREDIENTS	RECIPE DIRECTIONS

NOTES & RECIPE REVIEW

Serves	
Prep Time	
Cook Time	
Tools	
Temp	

Total	Carbs	Fat	Protein	Cals

RECIPE NAME:

Keto · Low Carb · Paleo · Vegetarian · Vegan · Dairy Free · Gluten Free

QTY	INGREDIENTS

RECIPE DIRECTIONS

NOTES & RECIPE REVIEW

Serves	
Prep Time	
Cook Time	
Tools	
Temp	

Total	Carbs	Fat	Protein	Cals

Recipe

RECIPE NAME:

Keto ☐ Low Carb ☐ Paleo ☐ Vegetarian ☐ Vegan ☐ Dairy Free ☐ Gluten Free ☐

QTY	INGREDIENTS

RECIPE DIRECTIONS

NOTES & RECIPE REVIEW

Serves	
Prep Time	
Cook Time	
Tools	
Temp	

	Carbs	Fat	Protein	Cals
Total				

Recipe

RECIPE NAME:
_____

Keto ☐ Low Carb ☐ Paleo ☐ Vegetarian ☐ Vegan ☐ Dairy Free ☐ Gluten Free ☐

QTY	INGREDIENTS

RECIPE DIRECTIONS

NOTES & RECIPE REVIEW

Serves	
Prep Time	
Cook Time	
Tools	
Temp	

Total	Carbs	Fat	Protein	Cals

53

RECIPE NAME:

Keto ☐   Low Carb ☐   Paleo ☐   Vegetarian ☐   Vegan ☐   Dairy Free ☐   Gluten Free ☐

QTY	INGREDIENTS	RECIPE DIRECTIONS

NOTES & RECIPE REVIEW

Serves	
Prep Time	
Cook Time	
Tools	
Temp	

Total	Carbs	Fat	Protein	Cals

54

RECIPE NAME:

Keto · Low Carb · Paleo · Vegetarian · Vegan · Dairy Free · Gluten Free

QTY	INGREDIENTS	RECIPE DIRECTIONS

NOTES & RECIPE REVIEW

Serves
Prep Time
Cook Time
Tools
Temp

Total	Carbs	Fat	Protein	Cals

RECIPE NAME:

Keto ☐ Low Carb ☐ Paleo ☐ Vegetarian ☐ Vegan ☐ Dairy Free ☐ Gluten Free ☐

QTY	INGREDIENTS	RECIPE DIRECTIONS

NOTES & RECIPE REVIEW

Serves	
Prep Time	
Cook Time	
Tools	
Temp	

Total	Carbs	Fat	Protein	Cals

RECIPE NAME:

Keto	Low Carb	Paleo	Vegetarian	Vegan	Dairy Free	Gluten Free
☐	☐	☐	☐	☐	☐	☐

QTY	INGREDIENTS	RECIPE DIRECTIONS

NOTES & RECIPE REVIEW

Serves	
Prep Time	
Cook Time	
Tools	
Temp	

Total	Carbs	Fat	Protein	Cals

Recipe

RECIPE NAME:

	Keto	Low Carb	Paleo	Vegetarian	Vegan	Dairy Free	Gluten Free
	☐	☐	☐	☐	☐	☐	☐

QTY	INGREDIENTS	RECIPE DIRECTIONS

NOTES & RECIPE REVIEW

Serves	
Prep Time	
Cook Time	
Tools	
Temp	

Total	Carbs	Fat	Protein	Cals

Recipe

RECIPE NAME:

Keto ☐　Low Carb ☐　Paleo ☐　Vegetarian ☐　Vegan ☐　Dairy Free ☐　Gluten Free ☐

QTY	INGREDIENTS	RECIPE DIRECTIONS

NOTES & RECIPE REVIEW

Serves
Prep Time
Cook Time
Tools
Temp

Total	Carbs	Fat	Protein	Cals

RECIPE NAME:

| Keto | Low Carb | Paleo | Vegetarian | Vegan | Dairy Free | Gluten Free |
| ☐ | ☐ | ☐ | ☐ | ☐ | ☐ | ☐ |

QTY	INGREDIENTS	RECIPE DIRECTIONS

NOTES & RECIPE REVIEW

Serves	
Prep Time	
Cook Time	
Tools	
Temp	

Total	Carbs	Fat	Protein	Cals

RECIPE NAME:

Keto ☐ Low Carb ☐ Paleo ☐ Vegetarian ☐ Vegan ☐ Dairy Free ☐ Gluten Free ☐

QTY	INGREDIENTS	RECIPE DIRECTIONS

NOTES & RECIPE REVIEW

Serves	
Prep Time	
Cook Time	
Tools	
Temp	

Total	Carbs	Fat	Protein	Cals

RECIPE NAME:

☐ Keto   ☐ Low Carb   ☐ Paleo   ☐ Vegetarian   ☐ Vegan   ☐ Dairy Free   ☐ Gluten Free

QTY	INGREDIENTS	RECIPE DIRECTIONS

NOTES & RECIPE REVIEW

Serves	
Prep Time	
Cook Time	
Tools	
Temp	

Total	Carbs	Fat	Protein	Cals

RECIPE NAME:

Keto ☐ Low Carb ☐ Paleo ☐ Vegetarian ☐ Vegan ☐ Dairy Free ☐ Gluten Free ☐

QTY	INGREDIENTS	RECIPE DIRECTIONS

NOTES & RECIPE REVIEW

Serves	
Prep Time	
Cook Time	
Tools	
Temp	

Total	Carbs	Fat	Protein	Cals

RECIPE NAME:

Keto ☐ Low Carb ☐ Paleo ☐ Vegetarian ☐ Vegan ☐ Dairy Free ☐ Gluten Free ☐

QTY	INGREDIENTS	RECIPE DIRECTIONS

NOTES & RECIPE REVIEW

Serves	
Prep Time	
Cook Time	
Tools	
Temp	

Total	Carbs	Fat	Protein	Cals

Recipe

64

RECIPE NAME:

Keto ☐　Low Carb ☐　Paleo ☐　Vegetarian ☐　Vegan ☐　Dairy Free ☐　Gluten Free ☐

QTY	INGREDIENTS	RECIPE DIRECTIONS

NOTES & RECIPE REVIEW

- Serves
- Prep Time
- Cook Time
- Tools
- Temp

Total	Carbs	Fat	Protein	Cals

Recipe

RECIPE NAME:

Keto ☐　Low Carb ☐　Paleo ☐　Vegetarian ☐　Vegan ☐　Dairy Free ☐　Gluten Free ☐

QTY	INGREDIENTS	RECIPE DIRECTIONS

NOTES & RECIPE REVIEW

Serves	
Prep Time	
Cook Time	
Tools	
Temp	

Total	Carbs	Fat	Protein	Cals

Recipe

RECIPE NAME:

Keto ☐ Low Carb ☐ Paleo ☐ Vegetarian ☐ Vegan ☐ Dairy Free ☐ Gluten Free ☐

QTY	INGREDIENTS	RECIPE DIRECTIONS

NOTES & RECIPE REVIEW

Serves:
Prep Time:
Cook Time:
Tools:
Temp:

Total	Carbs	Fat	Protein	Cals

RECIPE NAME:

Keto	Low Carb	Paleo	Vegetarian	Vegan	Dairy Free	Gluten Free
☐	☐	☐	☐	☐	☐	☐

QTY	INGREDIENTS

RECIPE DIRECTIONS

NOTES & RECIPE REVIEW

Serves	
Prep Time	
Cook Time	
Tools	
Temp	

Total	Carbs	Fat	Protein	Cals

Recipe

RECIPE NAME:

Keto ☐　Low Carb ☐　Paleo ☐　Vegetarian ☐　Vegan ☐　Dairy Free ☐　Gluten Free ☐

QTY	INGREDIENTS

RECIPE DIRECTIONS

NOTES & RECIPE REVIEW

Serves	
Prep Time	
Cook Time	
Tools	
Temp	

Total	Carbs	Fat	Protein	Cals

Recipe

RECIPE NAME:

Keto ☐ Low Carb ☐ Paleo ☐ Vegetarian ☐ Vegan ☐ Dairy Free ☐ Gluten Free ☐

QTY	INGREDIENTS	RECIPE DIRECTIONS

NOTES & RECIPE REVIEW

Serves	
Prep Time	
Cook Time	
Tools	
Temp	

Total	Carbs	Fat	Protein	Cals

RECIPE NAME:

Keto ☐　Low Carb ☐　Paleo ☐　Vegetarian ☐　Vegan ☐　Dairy Free ☐　Gluten Free ☐

QTY	INGREDIENTS

RECIPE DIRECTIONS

NOTES & RECIPE REVIEW

Serves	
Prep Time	
Cook Time	
Tools	
Temp	

Total	Carbs	Fat	Protein	Cals

Recipe

RECIPE NAME:

Keto ☐ Low Carb ☐ Paleo ☐ Vegetarian ☐ Vegan ☐ Dairy Free ☐ Gluten Free ☐

QTY	INGREDIENTS	RECIPE DIRECTIONS

NOTES & RECIPE REVIEW

Serves	
Prep Time	
Cook Time	
Tools	
Temp	

Total	Carbs	Fat	Protein	Cals

72

RECIPE NAME:

Keto ☐ Low Carb ☐ Paleo ☐ Vegetarian ☐ Vegan ☐ Dairy Free ☐ Gluten Free ☐

QTY	INGREDIENTS	RECIPE DIRECTIONS

NOTES & RECIPE REVIEW

Serves	
Prep Time	
Cook Time	
Tools	
Temp	

Total	Carbs	Fat	Protein	Cals

Recipe

73

RECIPE NAME:

Keto ☐ Low Carb ☐ Paleo ☐ Vegetarian ☐ Vegan ☐ Dairy Free ☐ Gluten Free ☐

QTY	INGREDIENTS	RECIPE DIRECTIONS

NOTES & RECIPE REVIEW

Serves	
Prep Time	
Cook Time	
Tools	
Temp	

Total	Carbs	Fat	Protein	Cals

74

RECIPE NAME:

Keto · Low Carb · Paleo · Vegetarian · Vegan · Dairy Free · Gluten Free

QTY	INGREDIENTS	RECIPE DIRECTIONS

NOTES & RECIPE REVIEW

Serves	
Prep Time	
Cook Time	
Tools	
Temp	

Total	Carbs	Fat	Protein	Cals

RECIPE NAME:

Keto ☐ Low Carb ☐ Paleo ☐ Vegetarian ☐ Vegan ☐ Dairy Free ☐ Gluten Free ☐

QTY	INGREDIENTS

RECIPE DIRECTIONS

NOTES & RECIPE REVIEW

Serves	
Prep Time	
Cook Time	
Tools	
Temp	

Total	Carbs	Fat	Protein	Cals

RECIPE NAME:

Keto ☐ Low Carb ☐ Paleo ☐ Vegetarian ☐ Vegan ☐ Dairy Free ☐ Gluten Free ☐

QTY	INGREDIENTS	RECIPE DIRECTIONS

NOTES & RECIPE REVIEW

Serves
Prep Time
Cook Time
Tools
Temp

Total	Carbs	Fat	Protein	Cals

Recipe

RECIPE NAME:

Keto ☐ Low Carb ☐ Paleo ☐ Vegetarian ☐ Vegan ☐ Dairy Free ☐ Gluten Free ☐

QTY	INGREDIENTS

RECIPE DIRECTIONS

NOTES & RECIPE REVIEW

Serves	
Prep Time	
Cook Time	
Tools	
Temp	

Total	Carbs	Fat	Protein	Cals

Recipe

RECIPE NAME:

Keto ☐　Low Carb ☐　Paleo ☐　Vegetarian ☐　Vegan ☐　Dairy Free ☐　Gluten Free ☐

QTY	INGREDIENTS

RECIPE DIRECTIONS

NOTES & RECIPE REVIEW

- Serves
- Prep Time
- Cook Time
- Tools
- Temp

Total	Carbs	Fat	Protein	Cals

Recipe

RECIPE NAME:

Keto ☐ Low Carb ☐ Paleo ☐ Vegetarian ☐ Vegan ☐ Dairy Free ☐ Gluten Free ☐

QTY	INGREDIENTS

RECIPE DIRECTIONS

NOTES & RECIPE REVIEW

Serves	
Prep Time	
Cook Time	
Tools	
Temp	

Total	Carbs	Fat	Protein	Cals

Recipe

RECIPE NAME:

Keto ☐ Low Carb ☐ Paleo ☐ Vegetarian ☐ Vegan ☐ Dairy Free ☐ Gluten Free ☐

QTY	INGREDIENTS

RECIPE DIRECTIONS

NOTES & RECIPE REVIEW

Serves	
Prep Time	
Cook Time	
Tools	
Temp	

Total	Carbs	Fat	Protein	Cals

RECIPE NAME:

Keto ☐　Low Carb ☐　Paleo ☐　Vegetarian ☐　Vegan ☐　Dairy Free ☐　Gluten Free ☐

QTY	INGREDIENTS	RECIPE DIRECTIONS

NOTES & RECIPE REVIEW

Serves	
Prep Time	
Cook Time	
Tools	
Temp	

Total	Carbs	Fat	Protein	Cals

Recipe

82

RECIPE NAME:
_____

| Keto | Low Carb | Paleo | Vegetarian | Vegan | Dairy Free | Gluten Free |
| ☐ | ☐ | ☐ | ☐ | ☐ | ☐ | ☐ |

QTY	INGREDIENTS	RECIPE DIRECTIONS

NOTES & RECIPE REVIEW

Serves	
Prep Time	
Cook Time	
Tools	
Temp	

Total	Carbs	Fat	Protein	Cals

Recipe

83

RECIPE NAME:

	Keto	Low Carb	Paleo	Vegetarian	Vegan	Dairy Free	Gluten Free
	☐	☐	☐	☐	☐	☐	☐

QTY	INGREDIENTS	RECIPE DIRECTIONS

NOTES & RECIPE REVIEW

Serves	
Prep Time	
Cook Time	
Tools	
Temp	

Total	Carbs	Fat	Protein	Cals

Recipe

RECIPE NAME:

Keto ☐   Low Carb ☐   Paleo ☐   Vegetarian ☐   Vegan ☐   Dairy Free ☐   Gluten Free ☐

QTY	INGREDIENTS

RECIPE DIRECTIONS

NOTES & RECIPE REVIEW

Serves	
Prep Time	
Cook Time	
Tools	
Temp	

Total	Carbs	Fat	Protein	Cals

RECIPE NAME:

Keto	Low Carb	Paleo	Vegetarian	Vegan	Dairy Free	Gluten Free
☐	☐	☐	☐	☐	☐	☐

QTY	INGREDIENTS	RECIPE DIRECTIONS

NOTES & RECIPE REVIEW

Serves	
Prep Time	
Cook Time	
Tools	
Temp	

Total	Carbs	Fat	Protein	Cals

Recipe

RECIPE NAME:

Keto	Low Carb	Paleo	Vegetarian	Vegan	Dairy Free	Gluten Free
☐	☐	☐	☐	☐	☐	☐

QTY	INGREDIENTS

RECIPE DIRECTIONS

NOTES & RECIPE REVIEW

Serves	
Prep Time	
Cook Time	
Tools	
Temp	

Total	Carbs	Fat	Protein	Cals

85

RECIPE NAME:

Keto ☐ Low Carb ☐ Paleo ☐ Vegetarian ☐ Vegan ☐ Dairy Free ☐ Gluten Free ☐

QTY	INGREDIENTS

RECIPE DIRECTIONS

NOTES & RECIPE REVIEW

Serves	
Prep Time	
Cook Time	
Tools	
Temp	

Total	Carbs	Fat	Protein	Cals

RECIPE NAME:

Keto ☐ Low Carb ☐ Paleo ☐ Vegetarian ☐ Vegan ☐ Dairy Free ☐ Gluten Free ☐

QTY	INGREDIENTS

RECIPE DIRECTIONS

NOTES & RECIPE REVIEW

Serves	
Prep Time	
Cook Time	
Tools	
Temp	

Total	Carbs	Fat	Protein	Cals

Recipe

87

RECIPE NAME: _____

| Keto ☐ | Low Carb ☐ | Paleo ☐ | Vegetarian ☐ | Vegan ☐ | Dairy Free ☐ | Gluten Free ☐ |

QTY	INGREDIENTS	RECIPE DIRECTIONS

NOTES & RECIPE REVIEW

Serves	
Prep Time	
Cook Time	
Tools	
Temp	

Total	Carbs	Fat	Protein	Cals

Recipe

88

RECIPE NAME:

Keto ☐ Low Carb ☐ Paleo ☐ Vegetarian ☐ Vegan ☐ Dairy Free ☐ Gluten Free ☐

QTY	INGREDIENTS	RECIPE DIRECTIONS	

NOTES & RECIPE REVIEW

Serves	
Prep Time	
Cook Time	
Tools	
Temp	

Total	Carbs	Fat	Protein	Cals

RECIPE NAME:

Keto ☐ Low Carb ☐ Paleo ☐ Vegetarian ☐ Vegan ☐ Dairy Free ☐ Gluten Free ☐

QTY	INGREDIENTS

RECIPE DIRECTIONS

NOTES & RECIPE REVIEW

Serves	
Prep Time	
Cook Time	
Tools	
Temp	

Total	Carbs	Fat	Protein	Cals

Recipe

90

RECIPE NAME:

Keto	Low Carb	Paleo	Vegetarian	Vegan	Dairy Free	Gluten Free
☐	☐	☐	☐	☐	☐	☐

QTY	INGREDIENTS	RECIPE DIRECTIONS

NOTES & RECIPE REVIEW

Serves	
Prep Time	
Cook Time	
Tools	
Temp	

Total	Carbs	Fat	Protein	Cals

RECIPE NAME:

	Keto	Low Carb	Paleo	Vegetarian	Vegan	Dairy Free	Gluten Free
	☐	☐	☐	☐	☐	☐	☐

QTY	INGREDIENTS	RECIPE DIRECTIONS

NOTES & RECIPE REVIEW

Serves	
Prep Time	
Cook Time	
Tools	
Temp	

Total	Carbs	Fat	Protein	Cals

RECIPE NAME:

Keto ☐ Low Carb ☐ Paleo ☐ Vegetarian ☐ Vegan ☐ Dairy Free ☐ Gluten Free ☐

QTY	INGREDIENTS

RECIPE DIRECTIONS

NOTES & RECIPE REVIEW

Serves	
Prep Time	
Cook Time	
Tools	
Temp	

Total	Carbs	Fat	Protein	Cals

93

RECIPE NAME:

Keto ☐   Low Carb ☐   Paleo ☐   Vegetarian ☐   Vegan ☐   Dairy Free ☐   Gluten Free ☐

QTY	INGREDIENTS

RECIPE DIRECTIONS

NOTES & RECIPE REVIEW

Serves	
Prep Time	
Cook Time	
Tools	
Temp	

Total	Carbs	Fat	Protein	Cals

Recipe

94

RECIPE NAME:
_____

| Keto | Low Carb | Paleo | Vegetarian | Vegan | Dairy Free | Gluten Free |
| ☐ | ☐ | ☐ | ☐ | ☐ | ☐ | ☐ |

QTY	INGREDIENTS	RECIPE DIRECTIONS

NOTES & RECIPE REVIEW

Serves	
Prep Time	
Cook Time	
Tools	
Temp	

Total	Carbs	Fat	Protein	Cals

95

RECIPE NAME:

Keto	Low Carb	Paleo	Vegetarian	Vegan	Dairy Free	Gluten Free
☐	☐	☐	☐	☐	☐	☐

QTY	INGREDIENTS	RECIPE DIRECTIONS	

NOTES & RECIPE REVIEW

Serves	
Prep Time	
Cook Time	
Tools	
Temp	

Total	Carbs	Fat	Protein	Cals

Recipe

RECIPE NAME:

Keto ☐ Low Carb ☐ Paleo ☐ Vegetarian ☐ Vegan ☐ Dairy Free ☐ Gluten Free ☐

QTY	INGREDIENTS

RECIPE DIRECTIONS

NOTES & RECIPE REVIEW

Serves	
Prep Time	
Cook Time	
Tools	
Temp	

Total	Carbs	Fat	Protein	Cals

Recipe

RECIPE NAME:

Keto ☐   Low Carb ☐   Paleo ☐   Vegetarian ☐   Vegan ☐   Dairy Free ☐   Gluten Free ☐

QTY	INGREDIENTS	RECIPE DIRECTIONS

NOTES & RECIPE REVIEW

Serves	
Prep Time	
Cook Time	
Tools	
Temp	

Total	Carbs	Fat	Protein	Cals

Recipe

RECIPE NAME:

Keto ☐ Low Carb ☐ Paleo ☐ Vegetarian ☐ Vegan ☐ Dairy Free ☐ Gluten Free ☐

QTY	INGREDIENTS

RECIPE DIRECTIONS

NOTES & RECIPE REVIEW

Serves	
Prep Time	
Cook Time	
Tools	
Temp	

Total	Carbs	Fat	Protein	Cals

Recipe

RECIPE NAME:

Keto ☐ Low Carb ☐ Paleo ☐ Vegetarian ☐ Vegan ☐ Dairy Free ☐ Gluten Free ☐

QTY	INGREDIENTS	RECIPE DIRECTIONS

NOTES & RECIPE REVIEW

Serves	
Prep Time	
Cook Time	
Tools	
Temp	

Total	Carbs	Fat	Protein	Cals

Recipe

100

RECIPE NAME: _____

Keto ☐ Low Carb ☐ Paleo ☐ Vegetarian ☐ Vegan ☐ Dairy Free ☐ Gluten Free ☐

QTY	INGREDIENTS	RECIPE DIRECTIONS

NOTES & RECIPE REVIEW

Serves	
Prep Time	
Cook Time	
Tools	
Temp	

Total	Carbs	Fat	Protein	Cals

Notes

Notes

Notes

Notes

Notes

Notes

CPSIA information can be obtained
at www.ICGtesting.com
Printed in the USA
LVHW100722110221
679017LV00004B/22